TreeHouse
books

1430 W. Susquehanna Ave
Philadelphia, PA 19121
215-236-1760 | treehousebooks.org

Strategies for Comprehension

Understanding Information for Classroom, Homework, and Test Success

Rich Mintzer

rosen central™

The Rosen Publishing Group, Inc.,
New York

Published in 2006 by The Rosen Publishing Group, Inc.
29 East 21st Street, New York, NY 10010

Copyright © 2006 by The Rosen Publishing Group, Inc.

First Edition

Library of Congress Cataloging-in-Publication Data

Mintzer, Richard.
Strategies for comprehension : understanding information for classroom, homework, and test success / Rich Mintzer.— 1st ed.
    p. cm. — (The library of higher order thinking skills)
Includes bibliographical references.
ISBN 1-4042-0472-5 (lib. bdg.)
ISBN 1-4042-0655-8 (pbk. bdg.)
1. Thought and thinking. 2. Comprehension.
I. Title. II. Series.
LB1590.3.M493 2005
370.15'2—dc22

                                                                          2004027380

Manufactured in the United States of America

Contents

• Introduction 4

Chapter 1 • Comprehending by Converting,
Describing, and Explaining
Information 6

Chapter 2 • Comprehending by Interpreting,
Paraphrasing, and Putting
in Order 15

Chapter 3 • Comprehending by Restating,
Retelling in Your Own Words,
and Rewriting 24

Chapter 4 • Comprehending by Summarizing,
Tracing, and Translating 31

• Glossary 39

• Web Sites 41

• For Further Reading 42

• Bibliography 44

• Index 46

INTRODUCTION

I t's been said that people learn something new every day. If you think hard about everything you did yesterday, you'll probably come up with at least one new bit of information you have learned. Of course this doesn't mean that you comprehend it. For example, you may have learned that H_2O is a chemical formula meaning two parts hydrogen and one part oxygen. Do you comprehend what this means? Or are you just repeating the formula? Don't worry, if you don't comprehend the formula, you'll learn how to in a later chapter.

Comprehension is understanding the meaning or importance of information. It is also the ability to perceive, or take in, information and use it in productive ways. It is possible to know a concept without it. For example, you could learn a list of a dozen words in a foreign language but not understand what those words mean. When you first study the classic works of William Shakespeare, you might be able to read the words but not know the message in the writing. Today you can probably understand and complete math problems that you could not understand and complete a couple of years ago. Passages in books that you didn't comprehend a few years ago are now easy to understand and explain to someone else.

As you grow and learn, you will notice that you'll be able to comprehend more complex materials. This is how the mind develops. People first comprehend material at a basic level and then they build a greater understanding of more complex material as time goes on. Once you comprehend information, you can use that knowledge in various ways, some of which will be discussed throughout this book.

In the next several chapters, you will be introduced to techniques that can help you comprehend information. You can use these techniques in your schoolwork, homework, test preparation, writing, or any area in which new information is introduced to you.

Comprehending by Converting, Describing, and Explaining Information

This chapter covers the first three strategies that are designed to help with comprehension: to convert means to change material from one form to another; to describe means to provide the details of a concept; and to explain means telling someone or writing about that which you comprehend.

Converting Information

People often convert information from one form to another. They do so for several reasons. For one, you may find that by converting information into a different form it becomes easier to comprehend. For example, you may convert Celsius degrees to Fahrenheit degrees, or vice versa, because one or the other might be more familiar to you.

People also convert information from one form to another to fit a specific situation. If you had 100 pennies, you wouldn't refer to it as 100 cents. You'd say you had one dollar because people more commonly speak of money in dollars than cents.

Football is another example where information is converted to fit a specific situation. In football, a player may throw a ball 60 feet (18.3 meters). But you wouldn't say the player threw the ball 60 feet. You would say the player threw the ball 20 yards, (3 feet [.9 m] equal 1 yard) because the game is played in yards, not feet.

A typical conversion that is frequently used is translating numbers into percentages to make predictions, such as the outcome of an election. For example, you could say that out of 50 people polled, 33 were planning to vote for John Smith for mayor and 17 were planning to vote for Mark Jefferson.

Figure It Out

Your friend tells you he walks five city blocks every day to school. If ten city blocks are equal to 1 mile (1.6 kilometers), how many miles does your friend walk going to school? In this exercise, you have to **convert** city blocks into miles to get the answer.

You would then convert your numbers to percentages. Once you convert the numbers to percentages, you see that 66 percent of the voters you polled said they planned to vote for John Smith (33 is 66 percent of 50) and 34 percent said they planned to vote for Mark Jefferson (17 is 34 percent of 50).

By converting this information, you can use the percentages to more accurately estimate, or predict, how the 5,000 registered voters will vote in the upcoming election. By using the prediction that 66 percent of voters will likely vote for John Smith, you can calculate that 3,300 voters (66 percent of 5,000) will likely vote for John Smith and 1,700 voters (34 percent of 5,000) will likely vote for Mark Jefferson.

Converting numbers into percentages in this way is, in fact, how political polls are usually conducted. Pollsters determine the number of people voting a certain way. They then convert those numbers into percentages and use those percentages to estimate how the election will likely turn out.

When doing schoolwork, look for situations in which you can convert information to a form that is more familiar to you, such as converting meters to feet or Celsius degrees to Fahrenheit degrees. You

Figure It Out

Convert 5 degrees Celsius to Fahrenheit degrees using the following steps:

1. Take 5 degrees Celsius and divide it by 5.
2. Multiply that number by 9.
3. Then add 32.

Did you get 41 degrees Fahrenheit? If you did, you're right!

would do this so that the information is easier for you to comprehend and explain to someone else.

Describing Information

We've all seen television shows in which the detective asks the victim of a crime if he or she could describe the crime. To describe in such a manner is to set a scene with words, which lets others know what happened or what someone or something looked like.

However, when you describe, you give an account of something in greater detail than just naming the item or the person. It is the use of details that makes your description more fascinating. The details also help the listener better understand and remember information.

Descriptions don't have to be lengthy. Your knowledge of a topic, such as the solar system, could allow you to answer questions with very brief

Try It!
....

Do the following:

• **Describe** what the weather is like today.
• **Describe** what your house looks like.
• **Describe** what you had for dinner last night.
• **Describe** what your favorite pair of shoes look like.
• **Describe** what this book is about.

descriptions. For example, which planets have <u>rings</u> around them? If you said Saturn, Uranus, Jupiter, and Neptune, you're correct. Which planet has a <u>reddish glow</u>? If you said Mars, you got it right. Using the underlined descriptive words, you can come up with the correct answer.

Activities, events, or actions can also be described. Sportscasters describe the actions that take place on a football or baseball field. Their descriptions paint word pictures that allow you to comprehend what's going on in the game. Similarly, you could describe an activity in which you participated and paint the word picture for someone else.

When writing a report, term paper, essay, or creative writing assignment for

Write It!

With a friend, sibling, parent, or anyone you choose, try this exercise. On separate pieces of paper, **describe** an activity that you did together. Set a time limit of ten minutes to write your **description** of the activity.

After ten minutes, switch notebooks and compare your **descriptions**. Make two lists containing the **descriptive** words you and your partner chose. You'll be surprised to see how your **descriptions** of the same event or activity can include very different details.

school, description shows that you have a greater understanding of what you are writing about. Description also makes the writing more memorable to the reader. You could, for example, write, "We enjoyed our visit to Boston." But if you wanted to add more description, you would rewrite this sentence and include the underlined descriptive words: "We enjoyed seeing the skyscrapers, weaving our way through the crowded sidewalks, and looking at the historical landmarks of Boston." Which of the sentences is more interesting? Which one shows that you have a better recollection of your trip to Boston? Which will probably stick in a listener's head longer?

Explaining Information

There are a few ways in which people explain information. People often explain something to make it easier for the listener to comprehend. For example, you might explain to your little brother, who has not yet learned to read, that the giant "Do Not Enter" sign on your bedroom door means that he is not supposed to come into your room.

When you do this, you are explaining the meaning of the sign in a simple way that he can understand. A verbal explanation is more comprehensible to your little brother than the words on the sign because he can't read yet. Words on a sign are meaningless to him. What he understands is your explanation.

When learning complex information, you need it explained in a manner that you can comprehend. For example, when you first learn a scientific formula, it may be very difficult for you to understand. However, when it is broken down and each part of the formula is explained, you can understand it more clearly.

People not only explain the meaning of words, symbols, or phrases, but also ideas. For instance, if you thought of a way in which you could make your school safer, an authority figure might ask you to explain your plan. To explain this plan, you need to take your ideas and arrange them so that listeners or readers will better understand your vision.

You might suggest that the school would be safer if there were only one entrance open at any one time. You might then explain why this would make the school safer. For one thing, if there were a guard in the school, he or she would only need to watch that entrance rather than trying to keep track of several entrances. Perhaps in the morning only the front entrance would be open and in the afternoon only the back entrance would be open, since the back entrance is where the school buses arrive to pick up students. This is how you would explain the reasoning behind your plan.

There is one last form of explaining that we've all had to do at some point. This is explaining to justify, or to give a reason, why something happened.

In other words, this is explaining why you were late to class, why you didn't do your homework, why you missed the bus, or some similar type of explanation.

A situation that you need to justify requires you to put together a series of events as a means of explaining why something happened. You might explain that your <u>alarm didn't go off</u>, and when you woke up it was five minutes before the bus arrived. You got dressed quickly but <u>could not find your shoes</u>. By the time you found them the <u>bus had already left</u>. In this situation, you are explaining the series of events, which are underlined, that led you to miss the bus.

Write It!
Explain in a few sentences ways that you think you could make your school safer. In order to effectively **explain** your plan, you'll have to organize your thoughts. What are the changes you would like to make? What is the reasoning behind making these changes?

Of course, this type of explanation does not have to be negative. You can explain how you came to win an award or how you saved someone from injury. You could also use the same method of piecing information together to explain how you solved a math problem or a scientific experiment.

Try It!

Try the following exercises:

- **Explain** the meaning of a vocabulary word you recently learned.
- **Explain** a dream you recently had and what you think it means.
- **Explain** the series of events that led to the Revolutionary War.
- **Explain** how to make scrambled eggs.
- **Explain** the rules of your house.

Explaining is an important part of your schoolwork for a couple of important reasons. First, by explaining, you can trace the steps you took to find an answer or solve a problem. This will help you remember the process you used for future problem-solving. Also, by explaining how you arrived at an answer, if there is a mistake made, you will be able to find out exactly where the mistake was made. Therefore, you should always either explain your work in school or be ready to do so if asked.

Comprehending by Interpreting, Paraphrasing, and Putting in Order

When people interpret, they seek out the deeper meaning behind what they are reading or hearing. Paraphrasing is combining your own words with those you have read or heard. Putting in order is arranging items in a logical sequence. Take a closer look at interpreting, paraphrasing, and putting in order.

Interpreting Information

We've all heard of interpreters. There are many interpreters working at the United Nations. They help dignitaries and representatives of various nations by translating their words into other languages. This allows the delegates to be understood by their UN colleagues who speak other languages. This is one definition of the word interpret: translating the meaning of information into a form that is comprehensible to the listener.

However, people also interpret meaning in other ways. For example, you might read a story or a poem, hear a song, or see a painting and not know for sure what the author, poet, musician, or artist meant by the work. If you think about the material carefully, you can begin to make sense of the words or pictures. Your interpretation of the material will come from your own understanding of what you are reading, hearing, or seeing.

When a detective pieces together the clues of a case, he or she is logically forming his or her interpretation of how a crime took place. Be the detective and look for elements that go together in a logical manner when answering questions when

Try It!

Try to **interpret** what creature the poet and inventor of the detective story Edgar Allan Poe is referring to in this poem:

"Then this ebony bird beguiling my sad fancy into smiling,
By the grave and stern decorum of the countenance it wore."

Interpreting from the underlined descriptions, you might guess that the bird Poe is describing is a raven. The poem is titled, appropriately, "The Raven."

you study, while doing homework, or while taking tests. Then see if you can come up with the meaning behind the material in front of you.

When doing school assignments, you may be asked to interpret the feelings or actions of characters in a book. By using your own interpretations as you study, you can be more aware of your thinking process when you read. In addition, you can use your own interpretation of school material to come up with questions that you have, which can be discussed in class or which you can look up while working on an assignment.

Paraphrasing Information

To paraphrase is to restate a text or passage in a way you can easily understand. Paraphrasing is a way of saying or writing something that has been said before, but in your own words. You are keeping the meaning of what has been written or said, but expressing it in a different, clearer way.

Before you can paraphrase, you first need to understand the meaning of what you are reading or hearing. If you are reading a book about the solar system and you understand how Mars orbits the Sun, you can then paraphrase the concept so it is easier for you to remember on class assignments and tests.

People paraphrase all of the time. For example, someone might give you directions to the

---

local mall by telling you to go about half a mile down Main Street and make a left turn onto Maple Street. You might, in turn, tell someone who asks you for the same directions to go five blocks down Main Street, past the A&P and Home Depot, and then turn left when they see the white church on the corner of Maple. These are the same directions, except you paraphrased by adding landmarks, which are underlined.

Often, while doing research for class work or homework, you will find information that is perfect for your essay or report. You cannot use the words

---

Write It!

On a separate piece of paper, try to **paraphrase** the following paragraph:

In the early sixteenth century, Europe was in turmoil. The Protestant Reformation, which took place from the early 1500s to the late 1600s, began when a group of people (later called Protestants) voiced their belief that the Roman Catholic Church was corrupt. This led to religious wars between the Protestants and the Roman Catholics. The Middle Ages was also ending in Europe at that time. This had been a time of great political and religious chaos, brought on by continuous fighting that scattered the people. As the Middle Ages ended, nation states in England, France, Spain, and Portugal emerged from the chaos.

18

Strategies for Comprehension

that are written by someone else, but you can paraphrase the ideas behind those words and explain in your own words what is being expressed.

Test questions often paraphrase the material you have already studied in class. This is done to test whether you understand the material and are not just repeating the words as you read them. So by learning to paraphrase and comprehend paraphrased material, you will perform better on class assignments.

Answer It!

The Greek God Zeus was married to Hera, and he had a child named Herakles. Hera, however, was not the child's mother. The mother was a woman named Alcmene.

Which statement is correct?

A) Herakles's parents were Zeus and Hera.
B) Herakles's parents were Zeus and Alcmene.
C) Herakles's parents were Justin and Brittany.

"B" is the correct answer. Nowhere in the information did it say outright who Herakles's parents were, though you can conclude who they were by **paraphrasing** the information.

When you are introduced to new material, try paraphrasing it as a means of studying for tests. Read, write, or say information in another form rather than using the same words that are on the page. By doing this, you will have a better grasp of the information you're learning.

Putting Information in Order

When you put information in order, you arrange it in a sequence that makes sense to you. There are, however, numerous sequences in which items can be arranged. For example, if you were asked to put historical events in chronological order, you would list the events according to the dates on which they occurred. You might also be asked to list the same historical events in order of importance.

Try It!

Put the following events in **order**:

1) Jennifer graduates from kindergarten.
2) Jennifer retires from her job.
3) Jennifer celebrates her tenth birthday.
4) Jennifer gets her driver's license.
5) Jennifer celebrates her fortieth birthday.

When putting information in order, individual items are categorized to show an order, such as tallest to shortest, largest to smallest, best selling book to worst selling book, and so on. However, certain types of lists require that you put information in a particular order because the steps affect one another. For example, if you were making French toast, you would first break the eggs into a shallow mixing bowl. Then you would add some milk. Next you would mix the eggs and milk together to make the batter. After that you would heat up a pan and add butter. Finally, you would dip the bread in the batter and place it in the pan with the heated butter. If you follow this sequence in order you can make french toast.

If you changed the order of these steps and started by heating the butter in the pan, and then dipped the bread in milk and added the eggs next, you would not have French toast. Each step affects the next step.

The writing process also requires that you put ideas in order. An outline for a story, an article, or even a book is an ordered list of what the reader can expect to see. It helps the writer organize his or her thoughts and know which area to focus attention on next. You see ordered lists all the time. The table of contents in the front of this book tells you the order of subjects and where to find them in this book.

Try It!

Sometimes by placing words in a certain order, you can see a logical progression of the words listed. Place the following words in chronological order to describe Sally's maturation process.

1) Toddler
2) Teenager
3) Adult
4) Infant
5) Preteen
6) Newborn
7) Young adult
8) Child

When studying, see if putting items in order can help you find a pattern or sequence that makes it easier to learn more about how a process occurs. There are several ways in which putting things in order can be helpful when studying. For example, if you were studying the Wright brothers and you had a list of facts including that they patented the airplane, owned a bicycle shop, invented the airplane, and flew their test flights at Kitty Hawk, North Carolina, you might want to put the facts in a descending order of importance, as in the following:

1) Invented the first airplane

2) Patented the airplane

3) Flew their test flights at Kitty Hawk, North Carolina

4) Owned a bicycle shop

When you study for a test, you can focus more attention on remembering the more important items at the top of your list. Typically, you'll have a much longer list than four items.

Another way in which putting things in order can help you in school is by formulating a timeline of events. For example, if your teacher wanted you to learn how a war started, you would get a picture of how the two nations became enemies by looking at the events, in order, that took place leading up to the fighting.

Also, putting information in order can make it easier for you to locate that information. For example, if you have facts on ten different subjects, you'll be able to find what you are looking for more easily if you put them in alphabetical order.

Chapter 3

Comprehending by Restating, Retelling in Your Own Words, and Rewriting

Restating is similar to paraphrasing. You state something again in a new form for clarity. When you retell in your own words, you typically tell a story as you see it. Rewriting is improving upon your original written work in some manner. In this chapter, you'll see how these concepts can help you improve your comprehension in school.

Restating Information

To restate is to state information in a new form. Restating is similar to paraphrasing. When you paraphrase, however, you include a combination of your own words and those that you read or heard. When you restate, you typically use most of the original wording in a new order or way.

The mere act of restating information the way it appears before you in your own words can help you better comprehend the information. Haven't you ever repeated something, and it seemed clearer the second time you said it?

Often, you will restate a question in your answer. An example would be:

What state capital has the largest population? The state capital with the largest population is Boston, the capital of Massachusetts.

A more complex example might include a series of questions or a list of data that needs to be included in an essay or report. By restating the key information asked or listed, you can maintain a sense of order as you write.

Did You Know?

To **restate** something effectively in a new form, you need to:

• Read it carefully.

• Look at the meaning of the words.

• Look at the overall meaning of the information.

• Compose the same statement or written passage in a new manner that does not change the meaning.

The ability to restate something you've learned, or say it in a different manner, becomes more important when you take tests or do homework assignments. It shows that you have learned the information in such a manner that you not only can repeat what you've learned, but also reorganize it.

Retelling Information in Your Own Words

To retell information in your own words is to explain, describe, or create a story as you saw it without using other material as a frame of reference. In other words, it is not restating or paraphrasing someone else's words but using your own words to tell the story.

The reason you retell information in your own words is so that you are not influenced by what other people have written or said. The idea is to express your own thoughts or knowledge of the material as you see

Write It!

When studying or reading a book, close the book and write down what the chapter or passage is about. You might also ask classmates, parents, friends, or siblings to select a topic that you are studying or story you are reading, and then, with the book closed, tell the other person about it **in your own words.**

fit. By retelling something in your own words, you spend less time trying to recall the words and phrases that you have read or studied. Instead, you focus greater attention on providing the events of the story as you recall them.

Before you can retell a story or impart information in your own words, you first need to organize your thoughts. Decide which points are most important and in what order you want to include them. If, for example, you were asked to retell in your own words the story of the *Titanic*, the British luxury liner that sank in 1912, you could call upon information you have learned in class, from books, or even from the movie *Titanic* to describe the ship's fateful journey.

When you retell a story or passage in your own words, you have the opportunity to elaborate on the parts of a story that you find most important, while recounting all of the key elements of the story.

Rewriting Information

To rewrite is to write information more than once in a different and improved form. Rewriting is an important part of the writing process and you can be sure that the books, articles, and stories you read in school and on your own have been rewritten before being published. In fact, most of the work you are asked to do for school needs to be rewritten in some way at least once.

Did You Know?

There are various reasons why people **rewrite** material. For example, people rewrite to:

- Make their written material clearer.

- Include additional information.

- Delete unnecessary material.

- Correct grammar, spelling, and punctuation.

- Use the written material for a different purpose.

- Restructure the order of the material.

- Elaborate on the material.

- Paint a more vivid word picture.

- Change the tone of the material (i.e., make it funnier or more serious).

One of the tricks to rewriting is to not fall in love with what you originally wrote so much that you don't want to change it. Everything can be changed and possibly improved upon. As you read your writing prior to your rewrite, you will probably see places where you want to change the information.

Many people think of rewriting as a chore. But it can be a way of taking what you wrote and making it better. Therefore, you can also see it as a challenge. Can you make your work better? Can you make it clearer? Can you better suit your writing to your audience? It's all a matter of believing in your abilities as a writer. The biggest excuse for not wanting to rewrite is typically not believing that you can do any better. That's why you need to motivate yourself to sit down and try.

First, know what the goal of the rewrite is. Are you trying to make the work shorter to fit the number of words required? Do you want to make the story more interesting by elaborating on key points? Maybe you want to make your descriptions more vivid by replacing the passive voice with the active voice. Once you know what you are trying to do, look for places in the story where you can make changes. When you're done and you reread it, nine times out of ten you'll like

Write It!

Find a paper you wrote for school two years ago. You may get a laugh out of how much your writing has changed since then. Now, sit down and **rewrite** the first two paragraphs. You'll immediately see how much your writing has improved. You'll also see how easy **rewriting** can be.

what you see and be glad you took the plunge and rewrote it.

Rewriting can also help you learn because each time you read the material and consider new ways of writing it, you are thinking about it. You feel more connected with the material when you read it a few times and think about how you can explain it in a way that will be easier to understand. This may help you better comprehend the material in school.

Comprehending by Summarizing, Tracing, and Translating

In this chapter, you'll look at what it means to summarize material. This chapter also discusses tracing information back to its roots and translating material to a simpler form. By summarizing, tracing, and translating, you can better comprehend the information you deal with in class, homework, and daily life.

Summarizing Information

To summarize is to provide a review or recap of material. For example at the end of a speech, the speaker may summarize his or her main ideas. Often a chapter of a book will include a summary at the end. That summary reviews the key points of that chapter.

A summary can draw your attention back to the important details in a large body of work. A three-page summary of a ninety-page report helps the reader

> **Did You Know?**
>
> You see and hear **summaries** often, as in the following:
>
> • Sports fans tune in to hear a broadcaster's **summary** of a game they missed.
>
> • Newscasts **summarize** news stories that took place earlier in the day.
>
> • TV listings provide short **summaries** of the programs on television.
>
> • Scientists **summarize** the results of their experiments.
>
> • Book reviewers **summarize** the books they critique.

review the information that he or she may have missed or forgotten.

A speaker, for example, might discuss the new computer technology in your school. She might talk about when students can use the computers and the rules for using them. At the end of a twenty-minute speech, she might summarize as follows:

To sum up, I want to say once again that I am very pleased that we are able to provide all of our students with the latest in computer equipment. As I mentioned, the computer room will be available after school until 5 PM. I expect that everyone will follow the rules and regulations discussed here today so that we can all benefit from having these new computers in our school.

A summary, however, does not substitute for a full body of work. In other words, if you are asked to read a book and you read only the summary, you'll miss the details that hold the story together. You will walk away with only the general idea of the story.

Write It!

Summarize the following paragraph by rewriting it and including only the most important information:

Over the summer, Mark went to Camp Evergreen. He met many friends and participated in many activities during the day. Mark liked fishing most of all. He had been fishing since he was little and was very good at it. One unfortunate thing happened to Mark though. He broke his arm while riding his bike. This might have been a fortunate thing though. While he recovered he read a book that became his favorite. It was called *Through the Looking Glass* by Lewis Carroll. He loved the book so much that by the time Mark came home he wanted to be a writer just like Lewis Carroll.

This is not helpful when taking tests or doing school reports.

The best way to use a summary when you study is as a guide. The points mentioned in the summary are obviously important, and when you study the work, they will guide you to sections that you may want to spend more time reviewing.

When you write a report, an essay, or make a presentation, you should consider summarizing your work at the end. A summary leaves your readers or listeners with a reminder of the important points of your presentation. Also, while in the process of putting together your summary, you will have the opportunity to review your own work and make sure you have not left anything out.

Tracing Information

Tracing is following a concept back to its roots. To trace also means to follow the steps of development. For example, you might be asked to trace your family history or the immigration of a specific family from when they first arrived at Ellis Island in New York to the twenty-first century. This would require researching, or tracing, the background of your family members, including where they were born and how they relate to one another.

You might be asked to trace the life cycle of a caterpillar. Therefore, you would start with the birth of the caterpillar and proceed to trace the process of metamorphosis until the caterpillar becomes a butterfly.

Tracing something to where it began can be very useful. For example, a medical researcher might want to trace the cause of an illness, or the fire department would certainly want to trace the cause of a fire. Since you don't know how the fire started the way you know how a caterpillar develops into a butterfly, you would need to work backward and start with the fire. By finding clues, firefighters and investigators can trace the events or activities that took place going all the way back to the activity that started the fire.

By tracing information while studying or doing homework, you can better comprehend the material. This is because tracing allows you to

Try It!

Do a little research and **trace** how your favorite singer or movie star got started in show business. Where was he or she born? When did she or he first start singing or acting? How did he or she get discovered? What was her or his first CD or movie? How did the entertainer get to be so popular?

understand the origins of certain information. Using the earlier example of tracing your family history, you can better comprehend who your family is today by understanding where your family members came from. Similarly, when doing schoolwork, you can better comprehend the material if you trace it back to its roots.

Translating Information

When people translate, they change information they've heard or read from one form to another. Translating is different than repeating and paraphrasing, which is using your own words to explain something. When translating, you are using two separate sets of words like Spanish and English. For example you could translate the Spanish word "hermano" to the English word "brother."

Try It!
....

Jane is 60" tall. Bobby is 66" tall. Mr. Clark is 72" tall. Adding up all of their heights, how many feet tall in total are Jane, Bobby, and Mr. Clark? To do this, you must **translate** inches into feet.

If you calculated 16'6", you're right.

You might also choose to translate information from symbols to words. For example, H_2O is the chemical symbol mentioned earlier for two parts hydrogen (H_2) and one part oxygen (O). You could translate this chemical formula into a simpler form: water.

You may find that instructions often need to be translated into a simpler form. On a test, for example, you might break down the questions and translate the wording into more familiar terms so that you can answer them more easily.

When you translate information into a new context you take what you learn and use it somewhere else. Measurements from math and science classes come in handy when cooking or building. Learning how to measure square feet in math class will be useful when you are helping your mom and dad figure out how many square feet of carpeting to buy for your bedroom.

Conclusion

The strategies in this book can be used to help you translate knowledge into out-of-the-classroom situations. By translating material into everyday language, you open the door to new ways of thinking about the subjects you study. Using the strategies and skills in this book, you can improve how you comprehend new information and how you communicate such information to other people on tests, in reports, and through homework.

Most of the strategies are actually used every day. In fact, these last two paragraphs are summarizing (one of the strategies covered) some of what was mentioned earlier in this book. The key to comprehension is to have these strategies available to help you simplify complex material or to find a way of organizing what you have learned so that it is easier for you to recall it. The more you use these strategies on tests and while studying or doing homework, the more familiar they will become to you.

GLOSSARY

accurate Correct, without any errors.

active voice Writing in which the subject of the sentence performs the action.

beguile To lead by deception.

categorize To place into different categories that are grouped under specific headings.

Celsius Relating to the international method for measuring temperature.

chronological Relating to the sequence of time.

complex Complicated or difficult.

countenance An expression of mood or emotion.

decorum Orderliness or polite behavior.

ebony The color black.

Fahrenheit Relating to a system for measuring temperature that is widely used in the United States.

interpretation A certain explanation of information.

maturation The process of growing and becoming mature.

passive voice Writing in which the subject of the sentence is acted upon.

poll To question by means of a survey.

reiterate To say something again; to repeat.

significance Importance.

technique A specific method for completing a task.

vice versa Referring to a situation in which the order is reversed.

vivid Presented in a clear and striking manner.

WEB SITES

Due to the changing nature of Internet links, The Rosen Publishing Group, Inc., has developed an online list of Web sites related to the subject of this book. This site is updated regularly. Please use this link to access the list:

http://www.rosenlinks.com/lhots/stco

FOR FURTHER READING

Anderson, Lorin W., et al. *Taxonomy for Learning, Teaching, and Assessing: A Revision of Bloom's Taxonomy of Educational Objectives*. Upper Saddle River, NJ: Pearson Education, 2000.

Atwell, Nancie. *In the Middle: New Understanding About Writing, Reading, and Learning* (Workshop Series). Portsmouth, NH: Boynton/Cook, 1998.

Ernst, John. *Middle School Study Skills*. Westminster, CA: Teacher Created Resources, 1996.

Gerber, Carole. *Reading Comprehension: Grade 6 (Master Skills)*. Grand Rapids, MI: American Education Publishing, 1995.

Gilbert, Sara Dulaney. *How to Do Your Best on Tests* (School Survival Guide). New York, NY: HarperTrophy, 1998.

Jenson, Eric. *Student Success Secrets*. Hauppauge, NY: Barron's Educational Series, 2003.

Luckie, William, et al. *Study Power: Study Skills to Improve Your Learning and Your Grades*. Brookline, MA: Brookline Books, 1997.

Robinson, Adam. *What Smart Students Know: Maximum Grades. Optimum Learning. Minimum Time.* New York, NY: Three Rivers Press, 1993.

Rokakis, Laurie. *Super Study Skills: The Ultimate Guide to Tests and Studying* (Scholastic Guides). New York, NY: Scholastic Reference, 2002.

BIBLIOGRAPHY

Bartko, Janine. Interview by Rich Mintzer. September 14, 2004.

Bergman, Todd. "Bloom's Taxonomy on Learning." Retrieved November 9, 2004 (http://www.mehs.educ.state.ak.us/blooms.html).

Friedfel, Peggy. Interview by Rich Mintzer. September 12 and 14, 2004.

Maynard, John. "Bloom's Taxonomy's Model Questions and Key Words." Retrieved November 9, 2004 (http://www.utexas.edu/student/utlc/handouts/1414.html).

Omaha Public Schools. "Comprehension: Bloom's Taxonomy." Retrieved October 12, 2004 (http://www.ops.org/reading/blooms_taxonomy.html).

Pogrow, Stanley. "HOTS: Helping Low Achievers in Grades 4–8," HOTS: Higher Order Thinking Skills. Retrieved March 22, 2005 (http://www.hots.org/article_helping.html).

Teachernet.gov.uk. "Higher Order Thinking Skills." Retrieved March 22, 2005 (http://www.teachernet.gov.uk/professionaldevelopment/nqt/behaviourmanagement/higherorderthinking).

University of Nebraska-Lincoln. "Aim High: Bloom's
    Taxonomy Breakdown." Retrieved November 9,
    2004 (http://nerds.unl.edu/pages/preser/
    sec/articles/blooms.html).

INDEX

A

art, 16

C

comprehension
  definition of, 4
converting,
  definition of, 6
  examples of, 6–9
  exercises for, 7, 8
  in school assignments, 8–9
  value of, 6

D

describing
  definition of, 6
  and details, 9
  examples of, 9–11
  exercises for, 9, 10
  length of descriptions,
    9–10
  in school assignments,
    10–11
  value of, 9, 10–11

E

explaining
  definition of, 6
  examples of, 11–13
  exercises for, 13, 14
  to justify, 12–13
  in school assignments, 14
  value of, 11–12, 14

F

foreign language, 4–5, 36

H

historical events, 20, 22–23,
  27, 34, 36

I

interpreting
  definition of, 15
  examples of, 15–16
  exercise for, 16
  in school assignments, 17
  value of, 15–17

M

math, 13, 37
mind, development of, 5

N

new information, 4, 37

P

paraphrasing
  compared to restating, 24
  compared to retelling, 26
  compared to translating, 36
  definition of, 15, 17
  examples of, 17–18
  exercises for, 18, 19
  to locate information, 23
  in school assignments, 17,
    18–19
  value of, 19
polls, 7–8
putting in order
  definition of, 15, 20
  examples of, 20–23
  exercises for, 20, 22

in school assignments, 20, 21, 22, 23
value of, 20–23

R
repeating, 4, 25, 26, 36
restating
  compared to paraphrasing, 24
  compared to retelling, 26
  definition of, 24, 26
  examples of, 25
  in school assignments, 25–26
  value of, 24–26
retelling in your own words
  compared to restating and para-phrasing, 26
  definition of, 24, 26
  example of, 27
  exercise for, 26
  in school assignments, 27
  value of, 26–27
rewriting
  definition of, 24, 27
  examples of, 27
  exercise for, 29
  in school assignments, 27–30
  value of, 28, 29, 30

S
school safety, 12
science, 10, 13, 17, 34–35, 37
Shakespeare, William, 5
speech/speaker, 31–33
sports, 7, 10

studying, 17, 20, 22, 23, 35, 38
summarizing
  definition of, 31
  examples of, 31–33, 38
  exercise for, 33
  in school assignments, 34
  value of, 31–32, 34

T
test questions, 19, 37
tests, 5, 17, 19–20, 23, 26, 34, 37, 38
timeline, 23
Titanic, 27
tracing
  definition of, 34
  examples of, 34–36
  exercise for, 35
  in school assignments, 35–36
  value of, 35–36
translating
  compared to paraphrasing, 36
  definition of, 36
  examples of, 36–37
  exercise for, 36
  in school assignments, 37
  value of, 37

U
United Nations (UN), 15

W
Wright brothers, 22–23
writing process, 21, 25, 27–30

About the Author

Rich Mintzer is an accomplished journalist and author who has thirty-four nonfiction books to his credit, including *Coping with Acts of Random Violence*, published by Rosen. Mintzer's books have been published by New American Library, Putnam, Adams Media, Chelsea House, Macmillan, and other companies. He has also heavily researched strategies for learning and comprehension, including Bloom's Taxonomy and the higher-order-thinking-skills strategy used in many schools.

Designer: Nelson Sá; Editor: Nicholas Croce